THE ABC'S OF SLEEP

AMBER GILMORE

Illustrated By: Ghyvari

THE ABC'S OF SLEEP
Copyright 2020 by Amber Gilmore
Illustrated by Ghyvari

All rights reserved. This book or any portion thereof may not be reproduced or used in any manner whatsoever without the express written permission of the publisher except for the use of brief quotations in a book review.

ISBN: 978-1-7357165-1-0

Dedications:

To all of my nieces and nephews, thank you for brightening my life with your unconditional love.

To all of the families who trusted me with their babies, thank you. It has been an honor to help establish positive sleep habits and sleep routines for your little ones.

Love, Amber

C is for curtains, to close out the light.

F is for Forty winks,
just enough sleep 'til daybreak.

G is for Gently, that's how we rest our head.

H is for Happy, as we're sleeping in our bed.

I is for Imagination,
that keeps you up with ideas, sublime.

J is for Just Right,
when you're in bed on time.

M is for Mom,
who helps us to sleep away.

N is for Night,
the time that follows day.

O is for overtired,
when you're too tired to sleep.

P is for Pajamas, oh, what comfort they keep.

Q is for Quiet,
as this helps us to feel tired.

R is for Reading,
it helps you sleep and feel inspired.

S is for Sound Machine, as it shuts out other sounds.

U is for Underneath,
when the sheets, we are below.

V is for Volume, try to keep your volume low.

W is for Warm, warmth is comfort and it's bliss.

X is for XO,
a huge hug and a sloppy kiss!

Y is for Yawn, it's nearly time to sleep.

Z is for Zzz...
Now you've nodded off so deep.

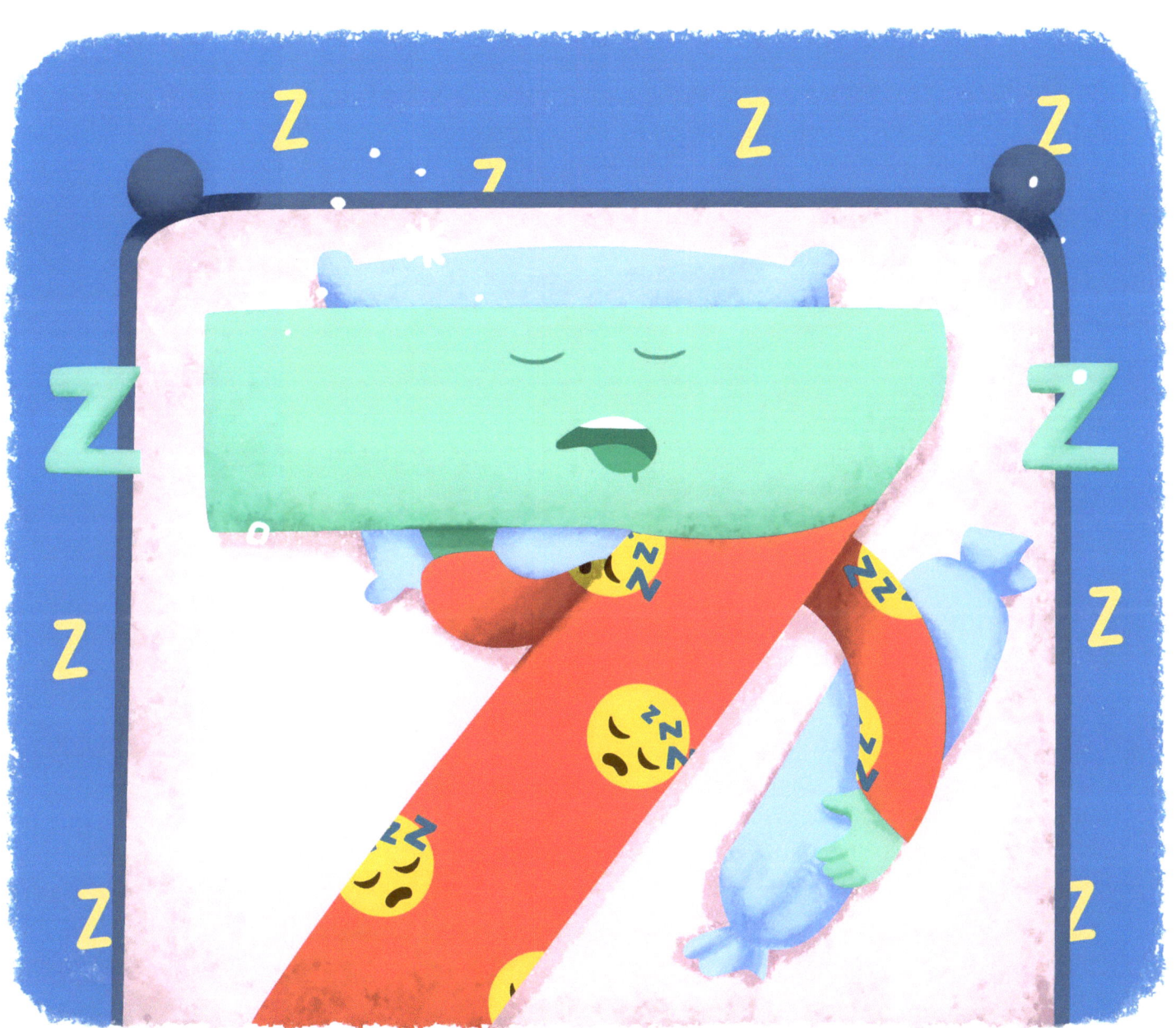

www.ingramcontent.com/pod-product-compliance
Lightning Source LLC
Chambersburg PA
CBHW041704160426
43209CB00017B/1736